BILL GATES

Success Secrets

—
VISIONARIES
WHO CHANGED
THE WORLD
SERIES

BILL GATES

Success Secrets

—
VISIONARIES
WHO CHANGED
THE WORLD
SERIES

George Ilian

JAICO PUBLISHING HOUSE

Ahmedabad Bangalore Chennai
Delhi Hyderabad Kolkata Mumbai

Published by Jaico Publishing House
A-2 Jash Chambers, 7-A Sir Phirozshah Mehta Road
Fort, Mumbai - 400 001
jaicopub@jaicobooks.com
www.jaicobooks.com

BILL GATES: SUCCESS SECRETS
ISBN 978-93-87944-81-7

First Jaico Impression: 2019
12th Jaico Impression: 2025

Content excerpted from
Top Visionaries Who Changed the World by George Ilian.

Page design and layout:
Special Effects Graphics Design Company, Mumbai

Printed by
Trinity Academy For Corporate Training Limited, Mumbai

Contents

Introduction

Few leaders in the business world are as revered or renowned as Bill Gates. His name has become synonymous with innovation and leadership in the software industry, enormous success, and of course, "The Richest Man in the World". Many look to Gates' story as both an inspiration and a blueprint for pursuing their own entrepreneurial dreams. This has been written with these people in mind, or those who are simply curious about the life of one of the most interesting businessmen of the last century. It is also deliberately brief, for those who hope to learn the most they can from the story of Bill Gates, but have little time on their hands to do so.

It offers an introduction to Gates, his business success and the lessons that we can learn from him. The key lessons outlined here are drawn from interviews Gates has given over the past 40 years, from the numerous blogs and articles written about him, and, most importantly, from the successes and failures on his road to the "Richest Man in the World".

On 28 October 1955, William Henry Gates III was born into an upper-middle class Seattle family. Gates was the middle child in his family, with one older sister, Kristi, and one younger sister, Libby. Gates' father, William H. Gates, Sr., was a prominent Washington lawyer, while his mother, Mary Maxwell Gates, was a well-respected teacher and local business figure, and held positions on a number of different company boards throughout her long career. Gates was affectionately known in his family as "Trey", a nickname that he earned from being the fourth to take the paternal name William H. Gates in his family, and thus the III-suffix with his name (Trey is a term commonly used in card games – a popular pastime in the Gates household – to denote a three). His childhood was a happy and carefree one, and Bill enjoyed a healthy and active social life. He participated regularly in various sporting activities, was a member of the Cub Scouts, and would spend summers with his family surrounded by nature in Bremerton, Washington.

When Gates was 13, he was enrolled by his parents at the exclusive Seattle Lakeside School, which was the perfect environment to nurture his creative and competitive spirit. Before this move, Bill had experienced some difficulties with 'fitting in' – he lacked direction, and was seemingly developing behavioral problems at the transition to becoming a teenager. At age 11, Gates developed rather rapidly intellectually, and began to also display a high level of emotional independence and rebellion from authority. He began to rebel against the control of his parents, particularly his mother. According to an anecdote told by his father, during a family dinner, Bill Gates Sr. threw a glass of cold water in Bill Gates Jr's face as a result of a particularly heated and bitter fight with his mother. By the age of 12, he was sent to counselling by his parents to address some of these issues. As a very clearly intelligent child, he was in need of greater focus and discipline that a school like Lakeside could provide. There, in 1968, he was introduced to his love of computers when the school fortuitously purchased a computer link terminal for use by its students. Although computers were still too prohibitively expensive for the school to own outright at the time, this method allowed the school to lease computer time for its students on a machine owned by General Electric via the link-up terminal. Interestingly, Lakeside didn't just permit their students to use the machine in a tightly controlled

"In ninth grade, I came up with a new form of rebellion. I hadn't been getting good grades, but I decided to get all A's without taking a book home. I didn't go to math class, because I knew enough and had read ahead, and I placed within the top 10 people in the nation on an aptitude exam."

—Bill Gates

environment, but allowed them a degree of relative freedom – an approach which Gates attributes to being responsible for his exploding interest in computers as a teenager. It was also at Lakeside that Bill met and developed a relationship with longtime friend and future business partner, Paul Allen. During this time, the pair got their first taste of business collaboration, working together to create a traffic counting program called 'Traf-O-Data'. Although this particular scheme wasn't remarkably successful, it laid the foundations for future cooperation between the two young entrepreneurs.

After doing particularly well on his SATs (achieving an almost perfect score of 1590), Gates was accepted to study at Harvard University. Although he was set on the road to becoming a lawyer – a path that his parents had actively encouraged from very early on in his academic career – his true interests lay elsewhere. He was particularly gifted at mathematics. However, on discovering that he was not Harvard's best math student, he quickly lost interest in pursuing this as his major. Instead, he diverted a lot of his efforts into the field of computer science. While at Harvard, he reconnected with his schoolmate Paul Allen, who dropped out of university in Washington and moved to Boston, where he began working for tech conglomerate Honeywell as a programmer.

United again, the pair eventually collaborated and conspired to form their own company: Microsoft. Following Allen's lead, Gates soon made the call to drop out of college and pursue his business venture with Microsoft full-time. He moved to Albuquerque, New Mexico and worked with Allen to establish the company there.

He later explained the sense of urgency that he and Allen felt in needing to pursue their business dreams, and his justification for leaving college in his final year:

> *"I loved college. It was so exciting to have conversations with lots of really smart people my age and to learn from great professors. But in December of 1974, when my friend Paul Allen showed me the issue of Popular Electronics that had the Altair 8800 on the cover, we knew it was the beginning of a major change. The Altair was the first minicomputer kit that came with Intel's 8080 microprocessor chip.*
>
> *For a while, Paul and I had been talking about how that chip would make computers affordable for the average person someday. We had the idea that this would create huge opportunities to write really interesting software that lots*

of people would buy. Once the Altair 8800 came out, we wanted to be among the first to start a business to write software for this new generation of computers. We were afraid if we waited, someone else would beat us to it.

It was a hard decision and I know my parents had their concerns. And while I would never encourage anyone to drop out of school, for me, it turned out to be the right choice."

Microsoft's big break came when the small start-up was commissioned by IBM to develop the software that was to be used on its machines. Gates and Allen arranged this by purchasing the rights to the third-party software that was to form the basis of the soon to be ubiquitous operating system, MS-DOS, and then selling the licenses to run the software to IBM, while retaining ownership rights. By doing so, Microsoft not only profited from the initial deal with IBM, but also earned royalty fees for each machine that the software was installed on. And when the personal computing industry really took off in the early to mid-80s, Gates and Allen were able to offer the same licensing deal for the same software to IBM's competitors, as the company held no ownership rights or patents to the operating system that they originally commissioned.

This business-minded stroke of genius was ultimately the deal that led to Gates making his early fortune.

After this episode, Gates became the sole representative of Microsoft when Paul Allen fell ill with Hodgkin's disease in 1982. In 1985, Gates launched the first edition of Microsoft Windows, which was to become the almost universal basis on which personal computers would be operated for at least the next 20 years. The following year, Microsoft went public on 13 March 1986 – a move which was incredibly well received by investors. The initial public offering (IPO) saw the company's stocks valued at a price of $21 per share. While the actual sale of Microsoft shares at its IPO made Gates his first million (specifically, a total of around $1.6 million), it was the 45% share of the company that he retained following the IPO that made him the bulk of his fortune. By July 1986, Gates' share in Microsoft was worth around $350 million dollars. In 1987, Gates became the world's youngest ever billionaire at the age of 31, and by age 39, Gates was officially the world's richest man with a total net wealth of $12.9 billion.

Gates continued at Microsoft in the positon of CEO, which he held until stepping down from the post in 2000. He was replaced in this role by Harvard friend and roommate Steve Ballmer, while Gates continued at the company in the position of Chief Software

Architect. In 2006, it was announced that Gates would be stepping down as an executive at Microsoft in order to focus his efforts on philanthropy through The Bill & Melinda Gates Foundation. Gates transitioned from a full-time to a part-time role at Microsoft by 2008, but retained his position as a non-executive chairman at the company. With the recent promotion of Satya Nadella to the chief executive position in 2014, Gates relinquished his post as chairman, and now holds the title 'Founder and Technology Adviser' at Microsoft. Gates' priority nowadays is clearly philanthropy, on which he spends at least two thirds of his time. He has funneled a huge chunk of his personal fortune through The Bill & Melinda Gates Foundation, which is dedicated to fighting "extreme poverty and poor health in developing countries, and the failures of America's education system", and is estimated to have donated around $28 billion to the foundation. Through his work in this area, Bill Gates is now not only known as the world's richest man, but also one of its most generous.

The rest of this chapter will explore the individual characteristics that helped to shape Bill in his youth and young adulthood, and would carry on to be an influence as he led Microsoft towards the position of being the world's foremost software company. Each section will take a look at one of the eight key traits and influences that have helped shape Gates' success throughout life: from college, through to his early entrepreneurial years, to the multibillion dollar success story he has become most famous for.

One

Risk

"Business is a money game with few rules and a lot of risk"

– Bill Gates

Even from an early age, Gates seemed to be aware of the need to take risks in life to enjoy rewards. Despite knowing that there could be severe consequences for such abuse, Gates and his fellow computer enthusiasts at Lakeside School in Seattle spent their time researching and exploiting bugs that would allow them to enjoy more computer time via the school's exclusive computer link terminal. At the time, the school purchased 'time' to use the General Electric owned computer through a special uplink, which was itself an expensive endeavor. Although this crafty strategy was eventually found out and Gates and the other implicated students were punished with restrictions on using the school's computer link during that summer, this was early evidence of an individual who had developed an appetite for calculated risk.

> As a young boy, Bill reportedly loved playing board games, his favorite was the aptly named Risk. The objective of this popular game is to move your 'armies' across a world map, attacking your competitors and defending your own territories, and ultimately pursuing the final goal of world domination.

The 'risk' in the game comes in deciding where to attack and how to spread your armies throughout your controlled territories. Of course, this risk is magnified by the fact that the outcome of battles is not necessarily decided by skill or strategy, but by the roll of the dice. Much like the board game that he loved as a child, Gates' life was one that has been heavily guided by calculated risk, as well as the invisible hand of lady luck.

Perhaps the first real major personal risk that Gates

took in life was his decision to drop out of Harvard to pursue his business aspirations with school friend Paul Allen. Education was a value that was always prized and revered by the Gates family. From his early childhood, Gates' parents encouraged the natural curiosity within Bill to flourish. He was the kind of child who asked a lot of questions, a trait which his patient parents helped to nurture and develop with their emphasis on the importance of reading and self-learning. At the age of 13, despite being great advocates of the public education system, Gates was enrolled at the private Seattle Lakeside School as his parents wanted to provide their son with the most optimal learning environment based on his personality. There was little surprise, therefore, when Gates was accepted to study at Harvard – a course which seemed to be predestined thanks to his natural ability and the encouragement of his parents. So when Bill took the decision to take a leave of absence from Harvard to found and run Microsoft, it was obviously a serious decision. He knew that his parents would be unhappy with such a course of action and, although they were taken aback by his decision, when they saw how much he wanted to pursue the dream of running his own company they offered him their full support. According to Gates, he told his father when he decided to drop out that he would be going back to Harvard. It took 32 years, but

Gates indeed returned to Harvard in 2007 when he was invited to receive an honorary doctorate degree from the university.

Much of the innovation required for a business to develop involves a good deal of risk, and this was certainly also the case at Microsoft. From the inception of the company in 1975 to the mid-2000s, Gates directed much of the product conception at Microsoft and oversaw some significant projects. Some of these were particularly successful, such as the company's famous contract with IBM that led to the creation of MS-DOS and the launch and reception of Microsoft Windows 95. However, others were less so, such as the poorly received Windows Vista and the company's lackluster success with its early foray into the world of smartphone software. What is important to remember, however, is that had Gates not driven the company to take risks with new products, Microsoft and its legacy would be a relic of the technological past, much like the Commodore 64 gaming console, or the floppy disk. Instead, thanks to the risks that were exemplified by Microsoft's changing focus in a dynamic tech world, it has managed to stay incredibly relevant by today's standards and is even continuing to innovate in certain areas ahead of its competitors. Interestingly, some of the reputational damage to Microsoft over time has been a result of the lack of risks it has taken on certain concepts. A clear example of this is the development of internet browsing software and related technologies. In an infamous quote from 1993 (the source is unclear), Gates is rumored to have bluntly stated that Microsoft was "not interested" in the internet. Later in 1998, he admitted: "Sometimes we do get taken by surprise. For example, when the internet came along, we had it as a fifth or sixth priority". This was arguably a valuable learning experience for Gates and his company. By isolating itself from the initial buzz of the internet and not taking risks to embrace the new medium, Microsoft paid in the long run. It will be surprising to see either Gates or the company making a similar mistake in the near future.

What can we learn from the risks that Bill Gates has taken throughout his life? First, his risks were always calculated. Whether it was leaving Harvard to pursue his start-up dreams, or taking risks on products and innovation, Gates was never reckless with the risks he took. There was always a clear goal in sight and there was always limited exposure.

Microsoft's endeavors have often been hugely impactful but rarely radical (best typified by the MS-DOS origin story, discussed further in the next chapter). Although many of Gates' critics cite this as evidence of a lack of creativity rather than a careful risk management, it is a method that has proved incredibly successful for him and his company. Even when he enjoyed huge success soon after he left Harvard to pursue his Microsoft dream, he could have easily returned to college had the venture fallen through. Before an audience of 1700 students at the University of Chicago, however, Gates reiterated the importance of education. He emphasized that students thinking of following his early exit example should only do so if they have a "very unique" idea that they are eager to work on and are supremely confident of their success. To paraphrase this idea and apply it as a general strategy in life, always analyze the size of the risk and the potential for return – if either of these factors point to an unpalatable outcome, then re-think your strategy.

“Success is a lousy teacher. It seduces smart people into thinking they can’t lose.”

—Bill Gates

Two

Lateral Thinking

"I choose a lazy person to do a hard job, because a lazy person will find an easy way to do it."

– Bill Gates.

Lateral thinking is a quality that has been highly valued throughout history, and has led to some of the most famous solutions to history's greatest quandaries and answers to some of the most perplexing riddles. For the average individual, lateral thinking can help us to achieve solutions to problems in day to day life, or in the longer term, and is an actively sought after quality that is often tested in job interviews for competitive positions. When it comes to thinking outside the box, there are few who have applied this as successfully to the business world as Bill Gates. While there are several examples of Gates' applying this style of logic to achieve his business aims, perhaps his most famous exhibition of this characteristic could be seen when he and then business partner Paul Allen were commissioned by the computing industry behemoth IBM to supply the operating system for their machines.

Following Gates and Allen's creation of the company in 1975, Microsoft enjoyed some early success with Altair BASIC, which was the foundation product of the company. This was the first high-level programming language available for the Altair 8800, a microcomputer that heralded the beginning of the personal computing age. Altair BASIC was the first in a range of programming language systems known as Microsoft BASIC, which became a common feature in personal computers throughout the late 1970s and early 1980s. At this time, Microsoft's debut project enjoyed hundreds of thousands of users. The success of Microsoft BASIC attracted the attention of the many in the fledgling industry, including the world's biggest name in computing, IBM. In July 1980, after IBM's efforts to obtain an operating system deal with the more established company Digital Research fell through, they solicited Gates and Allen to provide the proprietary software for their range of personal computers. The pair agreed to the deal. However,

“[Intelligence is] an elusive concept. There’s a certain sharpness, an ability to absorb new facts. To walk into a situation, have something explained to you and immediately say, “Well, what about this?” To ask an insightful question. To absorb it in real time. A capacity to remember. To relate to domains that may not seem connected at first. A certain creativity that allows people to be effective.”

—Bill Gates

they had one small problem – they didn't have an operating system to sell.

On 27 July 1981, Microsoft acquired 'QDOS '('Quick and Dirty Operating System', later known as '86-DOS') from Seattle Computer Products for the tidy sum of $50,000. This was to become the basis of 'MS-DOS' ('Microsoft Disk Operating System'), which Microsoft modified according to IBM's specifications before delivering the final product. Despite being more than competent software programmers, both Gates and Allen knew that the real opportunity of their deal with IBM had nothing to do with creating an original or revolutionary piece of software.

This would have taken years of development and testing, and cost an enormous amount of money in terms of dollars and man hours. Such a feat was beyond Microsoft's capabilities at the time. IBM needed fast results and having to wait years for a final product from Microsoft could have killed the deal. Though IBM was typically fastidious in its product research and development, it had come to realise that PC design and rollout depended heavily on quick turnaround times for the technology inside a machine to remain relevant. With this in mind, Gates and Allen saw the value of purchasing the rights to an off-the-shelf operating system which had already been thoroughly developed and tested for bugs, and had

“The first rule of any technology used in a business is that automation applied to an efficient operation will magnify the efficiency. The second is that automation applied to an inefficient operation will magnify the inefficiency.”

—Bill Gates

all the makings of a functional piece of software, for use on IBM machines after some minor tweaking. The real genius in the Microsoft/IBM deal, however, had nothing to do with the functionality of the operating system, but everything to do with the concept of software ownership.

In negotiating to charge a licensing fee for MS-DOS to IBM rather than selling the rights outright, Gates and Allen had gotten a hold of 'the goose that laid the golden egg'. The arrangement meant that instead of handing over direct ownership of the rights for MS-DOS to IBM, Microsoft was paid a royalty fee for each machine that the operating system was installed on. With this move, Microsoft also wrote a non-exclusivity clause into the deal with IBM, which meant that the company could sell the software directly to IBM's competitors. During the following decade, dozens of competitors to IBM sprang up in the field of personal computing, and almost all of their machines ran MS-DOS. The decision to push for this deal displayed an incredible amount of foresight and lateral thinking. Many in the fledgling PC industry, including IBM, firmly believed that the real business potential in the field lay in proprietary hardware. Microsoft, on the other hand, saw the money making potential of software and, through the establishment of MS-DOS, was able to dominate the industry in this area, and reap unprecedented financial benefits. This deal made the pair their fortunes, and catapulted Microsoft into the spotlight as the single most important software company in existence.

Many of the truly great minds in history have shown a high capability for lateral thinking, a talent which is particularly well-received in the business world. There is a fundamental advantage for those who are able to think laterally in such situations; this is because when we think laterally, we are able to think in a way that most people cannot. And when we can think in a truly unique way in order to arrive at solutions to complex problems, we have a greater chance of enjoying gains based on our ability to act in a unique and rewarding way. Gates, reported to be a deep thinker from an early age, has proven to be a master of lateral thinking, and offers in this trait another example that we should strive to emulate.

Three

Competition

"I can buy 20% of you or I can buy all of you. Or I can go into this business myself and bury you."

– Bill Gates to AOL CEO, Steve Case on Microsoft's potential for acquisition of the company.

The spirit of competitiveness was actively fostered during Gates' childhood in a family environment that encouraged and rewarded healthy competition. Whatever game the Gates children were playing, "there was always a reward for winning and there was always a penalty for losing." His parents encouraged his participation in sports and always rewarded victories, however small they were. According to his mother, Mary, Gates was "competitive in cards with his sister, races to see who could do jigsaw puzzles faster, ski racing, sailing – whatever. He wanted to do it well, and as good as the other folks that he was with." During summers spent with his family in a rented cabin on the Hood Canal in Bremerton, WA, Gates' competitiveness was again nurtured when he, along with family and friends, participated in their own 'Olympic Games'. Here, again, this spirit of competitiveness was obvious and actively encouraged. When Bill was enrolled at Seattle's elite Lakeside School at the age of 13, his desire to be more successful than others was further developed. According to Gates:

> *"Rigor absolutely defined my Lakeside experience. Lakeside had the kind of teachers who would come to me, even when I was getting straight As, and say: "When are you going to start applying yourself?" Teachers like Ann…One day, she said: "Bill, you're just coasting. Here are my ten favorite books; read these. Here's my college thesis; you should read it." She challenged me to do more. I never would have come to enjoy literature as much as I do if she hadn't pushed me."*

At the helm of Microsoft, Gates was fiercely and

famously competitive. He had a borderline obsession with being the best in the business and aimed to shut out any competitors. However, Microsoft's most famous rivalry was perhaps with fellow PC heavyweight Apple, and carried over on a personal level between Gates and Apple co-founder Steve Jobs. The history of the relationship between two of personal computing's biggest companies is long and complex. The two companies enjoyed a close relationship at first, when Microsoft worked to provide the productivity software that Apple's machine required to be competitive in the business world. However, the rivalry really began when Microsoft launched its first GUI-based (Graphical User Interface – as opposed to the text based MS-DOS) operating system in 1985, Microsoft Windows. Prior to this, Apple had the only GUI computer on the market with the Apple Macintosh. As Microsoft improved its Windows OS over time, it began to adopt more features that seemed to have a number of parallels with the Apple system. In 1988, Microsoft released Windows 2.0 which saw Apple launch a copyright suit against Gates' company, which went on unresolved for many years. Eventually, GUI-interface computing came to be seen as the only way to complete many personal computing tasks, which meant that it couldn't be copyrighted. Furthermore, Gates had persuaded Apple to license its 'virtual displays' found in its GUI operating system to Microsoft for the purpose of developing Windows 1.0. In 1992, Apples claim was dismissed, with Judge W. Schwarzer ruling that each of the above conditions nullified all of Apple's 189 contestations. In the long run, this ultimately meant that Microsoft and other competitors would be able to continue Apple's GUI-based platform as a model for the development of future operating systems. Microsoft and Apple had gone head to head, with the former coming out the clear winner.

> Although, Gates won in his fight against Apple, his desire to crush his competition landed him and his company in hot water in 1998, when Microsoft was charged by the Department of Justice with anti-competitive behavior. The company was accused of becoming a monopoly and engaging in abusive practices contrary to existing anti-trust laws.

These charges were filed on the basis of its handling of operating system and web browser sales. Specifically, this was to do with the fact that Microsoft, in its apparent efforts to snuff out internet browser provider Netscape Navigator, had bundled its flagship Internet Explorer web browser as a free piece of software with the Microsoft Windows operating system. In 1999, the presiding judge ruled that Microsoft was indeed guilty of monopolistic behavior and had exhibited attempts to crush its competition. As a result, it was demanded that Microsoft be broken up into two parts to remedy this issue, with one arm to produce the operating system, and the other arm, other software. Although this decision was overturned on appeal, this ordeal did a lot of damage to both Gates' image and that of his company. The former came to be seen as an industry bully, and the latter was viewed as the monopolistic giant in control of the personal computing world.

Gates' experience with Microsoft has shown both the good and bad sides of competition. On one hand, his persistence in going head to head with Apple resulted in the creation and development of one of its most successful pieces of software in Microsoft Windows. On the other hand, however, Gates' dogged pursuit of his competition very nearly led his company to the brink of disaster. From this we can observe that there are indeed limits to the benefit of competition. While it is the very spirit of competition that drives us to innovate and succeed, it can also become a consuming force which may work to our detriment if pursued to excess. Fortunately for Gates, he appeared to have learned his lesson from this experience without paying too high a price.

Four

Branding

"If I were down to my last dollar, I'd spend it on PR."

– Bill Gates.

When it comes to business and everyday life, paying close attention to branding is an indisputable key to success. Public perception is one of the driving influences of popularity, and Gates' experience with this – both in terms of his own branding and Microsoft's – has indicated just how important this can be. Gates is a man with a healthy respect for the importance of good marketing, once stating in an absolutist fashion "if you can't make it good, at least make it look good." During his time at the helm of Microsoft, Gates was closely involved with the company's marketing strategy from the company's inception. In the early days of Microsoft, Gates would personally spend hours planning and delivering the company's PR strategy. Initially, this involved spending a great deal of his time travelling long distances to pitch Microsoft products to potential buyers. Later, this role was expanded as Gates became the face of Microsoft by participating in a large number of interviews as the company began to enjoy early success. He went on to appear personally in print advertisements for various Microsoft products, and at the height of the company's success, in high budget television commercials.

In 2008, Gates appeared alongside comedian Jerry Seinfeld in a series of Microsoft commercials, which were seen as a direct response by Gates' company to the 'anti-Microsoft' Apple campaign from around the same period. Although the $300 million campaign received mixed reviews, it nonetheless highlighted Gates' own personal commitment to the value of marketing.

A clearer instance of Gates' personally driven marketing approach was the official launch of Windows

95. Long before the black turtleneck and Levi 501 jeans-wearing Steve Jobs' made Apple product launches the annual must see tech event, Gates poured huge resources into launching Microsoft's groundbreaking operating system with a huge amount of fanfare. Microsoft spent $300 million on the marketing campaign for Windows 95, and roped in celebrities like Jay Leno and the Rolling Stones to aid in its promotion. Following its launch, Windows 95 was a huge and unprecedented success. It has been purchased by over millions of consumers and has been run on billions of terminals. Most importantly, the operating system brought in billions of dollars in revenue for Microsoft. How much of its success could be attributed to its accompanying marketing campaign is hard to quantify. However, it is certainly reasonable to suppose that it had a significant effect in making it perhaps the single most popular operating system ever. What's more, Microsoft's Windows 95 campaign was perhaps the first major example of making the previously unexciting concept of tech release dates and carnival an entertainment of sorts. It set a model which many, including Steve Jobs and Apple, would later emulate as a core part of their own companies' marketing strategies.

Despite his readiness to embrace and exploit the great marketing machine, Gates has also been on the negative end of public perception, and in a

"Only a few businesses will succeed by having the lowest price, so most will need a strategy that includes customer services."

—Bill Gates

very personal way indeed. Over time Gates came to be viewed as the face of corporate greed and establishment wealth, which, as a figure who was named the world's richest man 12 years in a row, was a hard image to avoid. To make matters worse, there were several instances of public interaction where Gates was not portrayed as the most humble of characters. When he was called to testify as part of the United States vs. Microsoft Corporation antitrust lawsuit, he was perceived as being very uncooperative during the entire process. Gates gave terse answers to most questions, and displayed a lack of humility and a high degree of petulance, combativeness, and entitlement in his behavior. This was also repeated when Microsoft was ruled by the European Commission to have violated competitiveness standards, and was ordered to pay the single biggest fine in the history of the commission (and equivalent of $794 million) as a result. This episode of Gates' life yielded a valuable lesson – sometimes good branding involves not only active engagement through deliberate marketing campaigns, but also through the management of the public image during unforeseen events. Though Gates and Microsoft were certainly entitled to object to the anti-competiveness accusations that they were charged with, the manner in which this was done was arguably harmful to both the image of Gates and his company. Gates, however, did appear to learn from this experience, and took great efforts to appear as a more relatable 'every man' following this episode.

In an era of unprecedented levels of branding and public relations, we can all learn a valuable lesson from Gates' experiences. Though he has displayed a clear passion and vision for marketing his company's products, he has not been infallible in this area. Furthermore, while his efforts to directly coordinate and participate in Microsoft's planned PR campaigns have been particularly enthusiastic, Gates has experienced some difficulties with the more impromptu moments that come with being a public figure under intense scrutiny. Some have suggested that his engagement in the world of philanthropy was part of an effort to redeem his and Microsoft's reputation following its anti-competitiveness lawsuit. That Microsoft began to decline from its apex of immense popularity shortly after its antitrust trials is perhaps no coincidence. However, in any event, Gates' up and down experience with image perception highlights just how important branding can be. Life is a popularity contest for many, from individuals to corporations. Those who can present themselves and their interests in the best light possible will often have a competitive advantage in winning the support of their audience.

Five

Focus

"If I'd had some set idea of a finish line, don't you think I would have crossed it years ago?"

– Bill Gates.

One of the common misconceptions of being successful in the business world – or simply enjoying a decent amount of success through any venture – is the role of good fortune. Many people seem to place an excessive amount of emphasis in the belief that others have succeeded where they haven't, because others have had more than their fair share of luck. This is, in fact, a toxic attitude that breeds complacency and encourages laziness. The story of Bill Gates is one that is often touted as a 'right place, right time' success story – the kind where the stars aligned and the universe was in perfect harmony, and just so happened to generate the kind of luck that made Gates a very wealthy man. While there was indeed an element of this in Gates' success, it was also his dedication, hunger and focus that made his success possible, and is one of the reasons why he and his company profited immensely from the personal computing boom rather than a rival company. Though he came from a well off, upper-middle class family, this was of no importance to Gates when it came to his motivation. According to his father, Gates had an appreciation for the value of money from an early age. Even after Microsoft became a roaring success, he famously would fly coach rather than first class when traveling for business to spare the company's travel budget. He also exhibited a great deal of focus in his childhood when it came to learning. Gates was a gifted student with passions in many different areas aside from computers.

Perhaps the best example of Gates' focus is in the attitude he demonstrated in building and improving Microsoft, even after the company achieved monumental success. Gates was not content with a

Harvard degree, nor a moderately successful business. He displayed no apparent urge to relax his fiery ambition, not even after earning his first million dollars, nor his first billion. Instead, Gates is a man who apparently works to dynamic and shifting goals – for him, there is no finish line, only the next objective.

Gates' work ethic is famous, and was a quality that was instilled in him by his parents from a young age. In a recent interview, he claimed: "I never took a day off in my 20s. Not one. And I'm still fanatical, but now I'm a little less fanatical."He was constantly working away at his prized project in building his company to be the biggest and the best, and was simultaneously responsible for many different arms of the business in the early days, from research, to business development, to marketing. Whether it was developing new program ideas, negotiating business contracts or traveling long distances in to market the company to prospective clients, Gates' focus and ambition was evident in so many ways.

The hunger that drove Bill Gates' to become the world's most successful and iconic businessman is also the same hunger that compels him to work towards solving some of the world's most complex problems. Commendably, he appears to have brought the same level of intensity to this work that he exhibited in developing Microsoft. He regularly travels to regions of the world to raise awareness for various global health issues and to oversee and implement programs sponsored by The Bill & Melinda Gates Foundation. Gates also campaigns relentlessly for causes that the foundation targets, from vaccinations, to poverty, to education. He conducts this work in tandem with his current part-time role at Microsoft, which he approaches today with no less vigor than in the company's early years.

As one of the most obvious traits that can lead to success in any area, focus is also perhaps one of the most often overlooked. For a person to have a great vision or idea is typically not enough; though this can certainly provide the initial spark required for an endeavor to succeed, focus is the fuel that gets you to the finish line. One of the unique attributes of Gates is that his source of focus and hunger is seemingly inexhaustible. Success with MS-DOS was not enough, nor was Windows; indeed, he has carried the same attitude to his work in philanthropy, from which many in the developing world may benefit immensely. Focus is a rather difficult trait to create out of nothing. However, it is most likely to be exhibited in the pursuit of a goal for which you care deeply. If you feel that you are lacking focus in pursuing your goals, it is perhaps time to reassess your objectives and question whether you are pursuing what truly matters to you.

Six

Adversity

"Life is not fair; get used to it."

– Bill Gates

Though Gates' life is not exactly the kind that has been peppered with tragedy, he has nonetheless had to deal with his share of adversity, the trials of which he had to overcome to enjoy his success. Indeed, Gates has shown from his life that adversity isn't just something that we must overcome; instead we can use some of the more difficult experiences in life to help direct our future. For Gates, this was apparently one of the main factors that drove him to become one of the world's leading advocates for philanthropy and investment in solving the problems of the developing world.

All throughout his life, Gates was particularly close to his mother, Mary. Of their parents, she was the most constantly involved with rearing Gates and his siblings during their childhood. When she passed away in 1994 following a short battle with breast cancer, Gates was devastated. In a television interview, Gates' father recounted an anecdote of his son being pulled over by traffic police when speeding to the hospital where his mother died. Instead of wallowing in his own grief at the sudden loss of his beloved mother, Gates made a positive out of the sadness of her passing in stepping up his work in the area of philanthropy. His mother had always taught Gates and his siblings about the importance of civic duty and the value of 'giving back'. Mary Gates' philanthropic spirit was further emphasized in a letter she gave to her daughter-in-law on the day of her wedding, a mere 6 months before she died. In it, she reminded Melinda, "from those to whom much is given, much is expected". Following his mother's death, Gates donated $10 million dollars to the University of Washington to establish a scholarship in her name, as a tribute to her memory, her passion for education and her own spirit of philanthropy.

Microsoft also faced a significant challenge when Gates' friend and business partner, Paul Allen, was diagnosed with Hodgkin's lymphoma in 1982. Though Allen received radiation treatment and completely recovered from the illness, the experience reportedly affected Gates and helped to lend him some perspective in life. His friend's diagnosis also seemed to have the effect of focusing Gates, making him even more determined to drive Microsoft's success to new heights.

Gates also experienced several challenges when at the helm of Microsoft, particularly with regard to the anti-competitiveness cases that were brought before the company. Possibly the most testing experiences of his professional career, he navigated these hearings somewhat clumsily, as discussed above. However, despite this, Gates soon recovered from this experience and urged his company along a new path with a corporate restructure, and refocused much of his energy in his philanthropic work. It would certainly have been easy in such a situation to become bogged down by adversity, but Gates showed an ability to bounce back and take a new direction after the difficulties associated with his company's antitrust lawsuits.

Though, Gates' life is one that was not one of significant adversity, no life is without its personal challenges. It is important, therefore, to be able to deal with any adversity that might rear its head, whether that comes in the form of a personal loss or a professional challenge. Perhaps the most important lesson we can learn from Gates is that although we may experience challenges in life, our ability to use these experiences to create positives and draw new focus is possible. That is, it is still possible to find some hope in darkness.

Seven

Adaptability

"People always fear change. People feared electricity when it was invented, didn't they?"

– Bill Gates

With Microsoft, Bill Gates was in the fortunate position of enjoying great success and making big money relatively early in the company's history. From very early on, Microsoft was a behemoth in the world of personal computing. However, one of the difficulties of early success is being able to sustain this over time. For Microsoft, this has been possible thanks to the spirit of adaptability of the company that has very often been driven by Gates himself. Perhaps some of Gates' ability to adapt came from the fact that, as a child, he was encouraged to participate in a broad range of activities. During his time at Lakeside School, Gates excelled at a wide array of subjects including Math, Science, English, and was even a talented Drama student. His parents emphasized the importance of a broad and varied education, which was perhaps also shown in Gates' change in career aspirations while at college: from law, to math, to computer programming.

Microsoft's most famous early success was born from its adaptability when it was effectively drawn into the business of making operating systems. Before it was approached by IBM, who commissioned Microsoft to provide the basis of the proprietary software for its machines, the company had no experience in operating systems. It had created computer language programs such as Altair BASIC and its successors; however, this was a vastly different exercise from creating the software required for a personal computer's operating system. When Microsoft was in early discussions with IBM about the provision of ancillary software for its machines, Gates referred the company to Digital Research, a company that was already well-established in the provision of operating systems. However, when it became apparent the Digital Research were not willing to do business with IBM, Gates and Allen adapted the direction of

“A company’s ability to respond to an unplanned event, good or bad, is a prime indicator of its ability to compete.”

—Bill Gates

their company, and seized the opportunity to take up the contract with IBM that Digital Research had rejected.

> At times, Microsoft has shown some tardiness in adapting to changes in the tech industry, and it has certainly paid dearly on these occasions. The first example of this can be seen in Microsoft's approach to internet technology.

As stated above, Gates and his company were rather slow off the mark when it came to fully embracing the potential for engaging with this now omnipresent aspect of personal computing. When Microsoft decided to finally go down the path of assimilating its services with internet-based software, it was already too late. While it was somewhat successful in shutting out its main early competitor, Netscape Navigator, by including Microsoft's Internet Explorer with every copy of Windows 95 (a move which led to the anti-competitiveness lawsuit, discussed above), it did not take enough steps to embrace the internet's full capital potential. This complacent attitude allowed competitors such as Google to step in and dominate the internet sector. Despite spending billions on its online arm with services such as Windows Live (which pales in comparison in terms of internet traffic from services provided by Google), and recently purchasing Yahoo! for the significant sum of $44 billion, Microsoft's online presence has been rather underwhelming to say the least.

However, one area where Microsoft has exhibited a good level of adaptability is in its entry into the console gaming market. Though it would have been entirely plausible for Gates' company to rest on its laurels and isolate its success to the realm of personal computing, Microsoft's experience with the XBOX has been a resounding success. When the product was launched in 2001, it was a bold incursion into a field that was then dominated by the Sony Playstation. Since then, the XBOX has come to hold its own, carving out a loyal following of gamers and enjoying great success with the release of several generations and, in particular, the uniquely interactive XBOX Kinect. The Kinect broke sales records wide open for the volume and speed of sales of a consumer electronics item – 10 million units in just 60 days. Although this success came during the leadership of Steve Ballmer, Gates' nonetheless played an important role in guiding Microsoft's product development strategy during this period.

> Through his company, Gates has enjoyed varying levels of success when it comes to adaptability. Although adaptability has proven to be a game changer for Microsoft, particularly in terms of its early success with entering the world of producing operating systems, and the transition to the manufacture of gaming consoles from its traditional PC orientation, it has also lagged behind in key areas of development, particularly in the field of internet services.

One of the best lessons we can learn from Gates and Microsoft with regard to adaptability is that it is decidedly easier to adapt when things are on a smaller, less defined scale. This is one of the reasons that it was so easy for Gates and Allen to make the switch to producing operating systems early. One of the challenges of running such a large and established company such as Microsoft, is indeed the burden of previous success.

Eight

Humility

"We all need people who will give us feedback. That's how we improve."

– Bill Gates

One of the things that marks a truly great leader is a healthy dose of humility. This seldom exhibited trait can be misinterpreted by some as a weakness. True humility is in fact both a sign of immense power and consideration of that power. In the early part of his career, Gates was not exactly the kind of person who could be described as humble. It was apparent that he had immense faith in his company, his ideas, and his potential to succeed, something that he did not shy away from showing. Of course, given the then unprecedented level of achievement he attained from such a young age, it is surprising that Gates was as grounded as he was. Yet, despite the apparent brashness and self-confidence that he exhibited in his early days, Gates has evolved into a much more balanced individual in this regard, an attribute which is often accompanied by age and life experience. Although he certainly could have continued at the helm of Microsoft unchallenged, Gates stepped down as CEO in 2000, and relinquished control of the company even further over the following decade to spend more time focusing on philanthropic work through The Bill & Melinda Gates Foundation. One can only imagine how difficult this move must have been to make. Although some have questioned the extent to which Gates relinquished control of Microsoft during the tenure of his successor, Steve Ballmer, it is easy to empathize with the decision to give up executive control of the company that defined his success being rather difficult. While Gates' ability to hand over the reins of the company was itself admirable in its display of groundedness and perspective, the fact that he did so to focus on philanthropic work displays an even greater level of humility.

> Although Gates was dogged with the reputation of being the face of corporate greed for much of his career as the head of Microsoft (particularly during the late 90s and early 2000s), he has more than redeemed his reputation with his philanthropic work through The Bill & Melinda Gates Foundation.

The foundation was created in 2000 as a channel through which the couple could coordinate their philanthropic giving. Today, it is one of the world's largest private foundations, with an endowment of over $42 billion as of November 2014. The Foundation is "driven by the passions and interests of the Gates family"; namely, "alleviating poverty, hunger and disease in the developing world, and improving the state of America's education system." In 2010, Gates joined long-time friend and fellow multibillionaire Warren Buffett to create 'The Giving Pledge'—a drive which encouraged other billionaires to commit to giving away at least half their wealth in the name of philanthropy. So far, Mark Zuckerberg, Paul Allen, Steve Case and Larry Ellison are among those who have signed the pledge. To date, Gates has given away

“We make the future sustainable when we invest in the poor, not when we insist on their suffering.”

—Bill Gates

a significant proportion of his wealth through the foundation, around $28 billion dollars and counting. Gates is incredibly active in championing the goals of the fund and working to raise awareness surrounding the issues that it tackles.

Looking back to the time before he was consumed by work for the foundation, Gates learned how an apparent lack of humility can be incredibly damaging to one's image. The Bill Gates of today is generally viewed more sympathetically, perhaps due to his move away from Microsoft and his commitment to spending his fortune helping to make the world a better place. But when he was viewed primarily as 'the face of corporate greed', Gates was in fact reviled by many. Indeed, he did little to help improve this reputation when he acted with very little apparent humility when he testified before the hearing into Microsoft's anti-competitive practices, discussed above.

This final lesson from Gates – on humility – is perhaps the one that has shaped him the most into the man that he is today. On one hand, we can see from Gates' life how an apparent lack of humility can be a boon. Perhaps enormous success and complete humility aren't truly compatible, and Gates wouldn't have achieved what he did with Microsoft if he had been humbler in the beginning. However, we can also see from Gates' example that there are limits to this, and that a lack of humility can ultimately be damaging to one's reputation. Eventually, it seems, true humility is something that even the smartest individuals learn the benefit of with experience, and can become one of the most truly rewarding influences in life.

Conclusion

It is fitting, though perhaps unsurprising, that the world's richest man is also one from whom we have so much to learn. Thanks to the encouragement and values instilled by his parents, his own instinctive personality, and the people and events that came to influence him at various stages of his life, the eight traits and elements discussed above help to shape Gates' success. From the above exploration of some of these key concepts, we can see that the outcomes that Gates achieved aren't entirely down to luck. A range of qualities, from openness to risk, to focus, to the ability to think laterally were all instrumental in his success. Gates' ability to utilize these traits and characteristics in combination helped to drive much of his personal success.

From the above analysis of the influences on

Gates' life, which were the most important? First, it seems that a solid family life formed an excellent basis for him to become successful as an adult. Gates was very close to his mother, who instilled many of her core values and beliefs in Gates, including a dedication to philanthropy and a healthy respect for education. Gates' father had also been a profound influence in his life. Although he didn't follow through with a career as a lawyer, his decision to take the pre-law path shows that his father was a significant role model in his life. William H. Gates, Sr. was tasked with running the William H. Gates Foundation, the precursor to The Bill & Melinda Gates Foundation, which had the objective of putting laptops in every classroom in America. Furthermore, the fact that Gates' father continues to work closely with his son in an advisory executive capacity at The Bill & Melinda Gates Foundation highlights the respect that Gates has for his father, and vice versa. Gates' wife, Melinda, is also inseparable from the list of influential people in his life. On meeting his future wife, then a Microsoft employee, in 1986, he was quickly enamoured by her forthrightness, intelligence and independence. Shortly after they married in 1994, she helped to spur the couple's move into philanthropy and has continued to play a central role in driving this objective, now the most consuming element of the pair's lives.

Outside family, Gates has also had a few other key figures that have provided significant influence in his life. Warren Buffett, Gates' long-time friend and fellow multibillionaire, is counted among them. The two have rotated between the top spot of 'world's richest man' in recent years, and have also shared a commitment to 'giving back' much of their enormous wealth to help others. Aside from this common link between the pair, they are in fact close friends. Gates and Buffett first met in 1991 through a mutual connection, although both parties were initially apprehensive about the meeting. However, they eventually hit it off, and Gates had soon discovered that he had found a valued mentor in Buffett. In setting up The Bill & Melinda Gates Foundation, Buffett proved instrumental in offering Gates guidance. On this, Bill noted:

> *"When Melinda and I started our foundation, I turned to him for advice. We talked a lot about the idea that philanthropy could be just as impactful in its own way as software had been. It turns out that Warren's brilliant way of looking at the world is just as useful in attacking poverty and disease as it is in building a business. He's one of a kind."*

It is also clear that while Gates has had key influential figures in his life, much of his success appears to have been self-driven. This is particularly evident when you consider how early Gates achieved the bulk of his success, as well as the fact that even as a child, Gates displayed many characteristics that formed the basis of his later success. Indeed, many of the inherent personality traits exhibited by Gates have been viewed as the driving force behind his entrepreneurial achievements, and something that many budding entrepreneurs have attempted to emulate. His appetite for both risk and competition, his brilliant intellect and inclination towards lateral thinking, and his impressive dedication and focus all appeared in Gates from a young age, and carried through into his later years to help fuel much of his business success. However, we also know that Gates developed many qualities along the way that helped make him a more well-rounded individual, and one who was able to carry that initial success forward. His adaptability to change, handling of adversity and ability to be humble despite his enormous success, have all helped to make Gates a more nuanced individual with both more to offer and to gain from the world.

Meanwhile, Gates' individual achievements have been some of the most remarkable of the last century.

"Don't make the same decision twice. Spend time and thought to make a solid decision the first time so that you don't revisit the issue unnecessarily. If you're too willing to reopen issues, it interferes not only with your execution but also with your motivation to make a decision in the first place. After all, why bother deciding an issue if it isn't really decided."

—Bill Gates

No entrepreneur before Gates had ever been as successful in the sheer speed with which his business empire was built. His remarkable foresight (along with that of business partner, Paul Allen) to fill a gap in the market before the market even existed, resulted in one of the fastest accumulations of personal wealth in history, even to this day. Gates also helped to drive the change that has altered, in a very fundamental way, how we all live our lives. Though not directly behind the technology boom that occurred from the latter part of the 20th century to today, the enormous success of Microsoft helped the industry explode in terms of investment, innovation, and accessibility. Finally, Gates has done more than anyone before or since in terms of philanthropy. His commitment to spending a vast amount of his fortune helping the world's most disadvantaged overcome sickness and poverty is exemplary, as is his drive to encourage other 'mega-rich' individuals to do the same. In this regard, much of his impact is yet to be felt and will no doubt affect the lives of just as many, if not more, than in his significant life so far.

However, despite his enormous success and legacy, both from early and later life, we know that Gates is not infallible. He has made mistakes and bad decisions just like everyone else, despite his seemingly superhuman achievements. Good fortune did play a significant role in securing the quantifiable success that Gates has secured in his life. A person with exactly the same characteristics may well have failed in their entrepreneurial aspirations where Gates excelled, were it not for the crucial element of luck. Although we may not necessarily be able to emulate the same level of success as Bill Gates, we can take lessons from his achievements and apply them to ourselves and the pursuit of our goals – both in the world of entrepreneurship, and beyond. And though it is unlikely that any one of us will scale the same great heights as a result, we may still be richer for it – simply by understanding the factors that shaped the most unusual life of Bill Gates.

JAICO PUBLISHING HOUSE

Elevate Your Life. Transform Your World.

ESTABLISHED IN 1946, Jaico Publishing House is home to world-transforming authors such as Sri Sri Paramahansa Yogananda, Osho, The Dalai Lama, Sri Sri Ravi Shankar, Sadhguru, Robin Sharma, Deepak Chopra, Jack Canfield, Eknath Easwaran, Devdutt Pattanaik, Khushwant Singh, John Maxwell, Brian Tracy and Stephen Hawking.

Our late founder Mr. Jaman Shah first established Jaico as a book distribution company. Sensing that independence was around the corner, he aptly named his company Jaico ('Jai' means victory in Hindi). In order to service the significant demand for affordable books in a developing nation, Mr. Shah initiated Jaico's own publications. Jaico was India's first publisher of paperback books in the English language.

While self-help, religion and philosophy, mind/body/spirit, and business titles form the cornerstone of our non-fiction list, we publish an exciting range of travel, current affairs, biography, and popular science books as well. Our renewed focus on popular fiction is evident in our new titles by a host of fresh young talent from India and abroad. Jaico's recently established Translations Division translates selected English content into nine regional languages.

In addition to being a publisher and distributor of its own titles, Jaico is a major national distributor of books of leading international and Indian publishers. With its headquarters in Mumbai, Jaico has branches and sales offices in Ahmedabad, Bangalore, Bhopal, Chennai, Delhi, Hyderabad, Kolkata and Lucknow.

SINCE 1946